MW00973861

COLLECTAFACT™

WORDS AND PICTURES THAT WORK TOGETHER

WATER

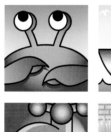
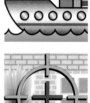

TWO CAN™

PRINCETON ■ LONDON

What's in this book

4 **Water over the world**
It's a wet and wonderful world out there!

6 **The water cycle**
Learn about water's journey from ocean to sky and back again.

8 **Water and the weather**
Rain, snow, hail, and fog are all in the forecast.

10 **Water pressure**
What does it feel like to be underwater?

12 **Making a submarine**
Dive into deep water with your own submarine.

14 **Weight and volume**
Find out how to measure volume in water.

16 **Floating and sinking**
Drop in for a tank full of dunking experiments!

18 **Shipshape and seaworthy**
Look at ships and boats.

20 **Surface tension**
Meet an insect that can walk across water.

22 **Separating colors**
Discover all the differen colors that make up ink

*All words in the text which appear in **bold** can be found in the glossary.*

24 All-purpose water
Learn how water is stored and used to make electricity.

26 Make your own water wheel
See water power in action.

28 Being water aware
Learn to look after the world's water supply.

30 Saving water
You can help to avoid a world water shortage.

32 Survey
How much water do you use each day?

33 Puzzles
Wise up with some watery work-outs.

34 Glossary
All the key words explained

38 Workbook
Here are note pages for your own use.

44 Questions and answers
Answer all your water questions.

46 Index
An easy way to find topics of interest

Water over the world

Water is all around us. It covers most of Earth and all the planet's living things need it to survive. We have to drink plenty of it every day. Our bodies are made up of about two-thirds water!

Water first appeared on Earth millions of years ago as a **gas** that came out of **volcanoes**. This gas, called **water vapor**, cooled down to form the oceans. Now water can be found as a **liquid**, a gas, and solid **ice**. Look around and see how many places you can find water in all its different forms. Then discover its amazing properties.

▲ When liquid water is boiled, it turns into a gas called steam.

▼ Most of the water on Earth is sea water, which is too salty for us to drink. This water is home to millions of living things. These range from tiny animals and plants called plankton that float near the surface to Earth's largest mammals, the blue whales that feed on them.

▼ When water freezes, it turns into solid ice like these icicles.

There are about 326 million cubic miles (1,500 million million cubic meters) of water on Earth. Water in the form of ice has even been found in deep craters on the Moon!

FastFact
Sheep and cattle can drink water that is too salty for humans to drink! Humans should never drink sea water.

The water cycle

Earth's water is hardly ever still. Water from the ocean travels on a long journey called the **water cycle**. As ocean water is warmed up by energy from the sun, it evaporates, turning into water vapor that condenses to form **clouds**. When it rains, this water flows into **rivers**, **lakes**, and **oceans**. Then the cycle begins again.

◀ You can see the water cycle in action in your home. Pour a little water onto a plate. Leave it overnight. In the morning, the water level has dropped a little. Where has the water gone? It has turned from liquid water into water vapor in the air.

FastFact
Only one-thousandth of one percent of Earth's water is found in the air we breathe at any one time.

▼ On a cold day, warm water vapor in a bathroom condenses on the mirror. Water drips down the cold glass like rain.

Water and
the weather

The weather is different all over the
world. Water plays an important part
in the weather and it can appear in
many forms.

▶ Tiny water droplets inside a cloud join
together to become larger droplets.
When they are big enough, the droplets
fall out of the cloud as rain like these
that have landed on a leaf.

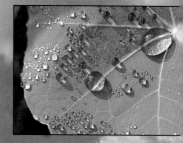

If the air near the ground has a lot of water vapor in it and is cooled, the water vapor condenses and forms a ground-level cloud. This is called fog.

◄ Sometimes it is very cold in a cloud, less than 32°F (0°C). At this temperature, the water droplets in a cloud freeze together to form tiny ice crystals. The crystals stick together and when the air below the cloud is also cold, the ice falls as snow.

◄ The air in a cloud is always moving. If an ice crystal is swept up through a cloud by rising winds, it can grow into a large ball of ice. This is how hail is formed. Sometimes hail can be huge. In 1970, a hailstone the size of a melon fell on Coffeyville in Kansas!

Water pressure

Have you ever tried to touch the bottom of a swimming pool? Sometimes, when you try, you can feel the water pressing on your ears. This is because the water has **pressure** which is pushing on your eardrums. As you go deeper, the pressure gets greater and your ears may hurt.

Try holding your head at different angles. You can still feel the pressure of the water because it pushes in all directions. If you want to try this at home or at your local swimming pool, make sure an adult or lifeguard is nearby.

▼ Seals always close their nostrils and ears when they dive deeply.

Experiment with water pressure

Ask an adult to help you make three holes at different heights down the side of a plastic bottle using the point of some scissors. Get a friend to help you with the next part because you'll need three hands.

With your friend, cover up the holes with your fingers and fill the bottle with water. Quickly take your fingers away. The water will spurt from the holes. Which hole has the biggest jet of water? Why do you think this is?

Making a submarine

Submarines are special ships that can travel underwater. They have to be strong so the great **pressure** deep under the ocean does not crush them.

UNDERSEAS DEVELO

...easy to make a submarine that dives
... surfaces just like the real thing. You
... amaze your friends by making it go
... and down without touching it—just
... magic!

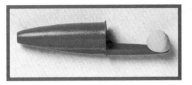

▲ All you need is a long, thin pen top, some
modeling clay and a plastic bottle with a
cap. Push a small blob of clay inside the pen
top to block the hole and another small blob
on the end. You may need to try different-
sized blobs of clay.

▼ Put the pen top in a bottle full of water
and screw the bottle cap on tightly. The pen
top will float near the surface of the water.
Now ask your friends if they want the pen
top to float or sink. You can control it by
squeezing the sides of the bottle!

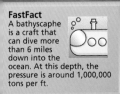

FastFact
A bathyscaphe
is a craft that
can dive more
than 6 miles
down into the
ocean. At this depth, the
pressure is around 1,000,000
tons per ft.

Weight and volume

About 2,200 years ago, the king of Syracu
in Sicily bought a golden crown. He was t
that the crown was made of solid gold bu
he wanted to make sure. The king asked a
smart man named Archimedes to find out
how much pure gold his crown was made
of without damaging it.

When he was getting into the bathtub,
Archimedes suddenly realized how he cou
check the crown. He was so excited that h
ran down the street. Unfortunately, he
forgot to get dressed!

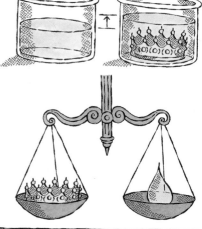

To check the king's crown,
Archimedes first filled a bowl
with water. Then he dropped
the crown in it and measured
the change in the water level.
This was the crown's **volume**.
Archimedes weighed the crown
and this volume of water to
find out how many times
heavier the crown was than
water. Then he compared the
weight of solid gold with its
volume in water to find out
how much heavier gold is than
water. He found that the crown
was not solid gold after all!

◀ Next time you take a bath, see what happens to the level of the water. Before you climb in, mark the top level of the water with a crayon. Now get into the bath and mark the new level. Look at the difference in height between the two marks. An object will push up the level of water by the amount of space it takes up, or its volume. You have just measured the volume of your body in the water! Don't forget to wipe off the crayon marks after the experiment!

this experiment to measure the volume a stone! Put exactly 17oz. (500ml) water into a measuring cup. Carefully t a stone into the measuring cup and easure the new level of the water.

In this experiment, the water level se from 17oz. (500ml) to 20oz. (600ml). he stone took the place of 3oz. (100ml) f water and pushed the level up.

One ounce is the same as 1.8 cubic inches (1.8in^3). So what was the volume of the stone?

Floating and sinking

Have you ever noticed that some things **float** and some things **sink**? Make a collection of things from around the house and guess which ones will float and which ones will sink.

▼ Fill a tank or bucket with water. Put your collection of things in the water. Were you surprised? Did you think that the heavy things would sink and the light ones float?

FastFact
On the side of a ship, you will see a line. This is the Plimsoll line, which shows the deepest the ship should sink under certain conditions.

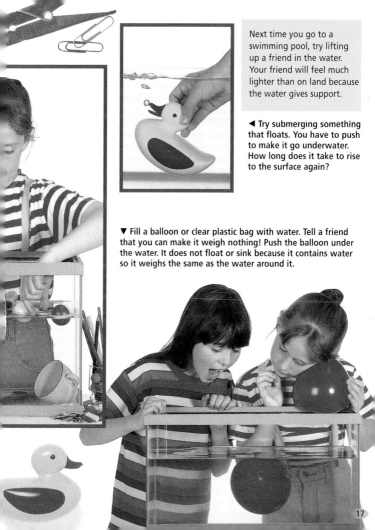

Next time you go to a swimming pool, try lifting up a friend in the water. Your friend will feel much lighter than on land because the water gives support.

◀ Try submerging something that floats. You have to push to make it go underwater. How long does it take to rise to the surface again?

▼ Fill a balloon or clear plastic bag with water. Tell a friend that you can make it weigh nothing! Push the balloon under the water. It does not float or sink because it contains water so it weighs the same as the water around it.

Shipshape and seaworthy

Ships and boats come in all shapes and sizes. See if you can design and make two different types of boat out of modeling clay.

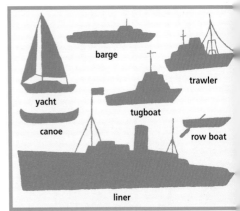

barge

trawler

yacht

tugboat

canoe

row boat

liner

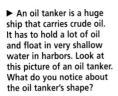

▶ An oil tanker is a huge ship that carries crude oil. It has to hold a lot of oil and float in very shallow water in harbors. Look at this picture of an oil tanker. What do you notice about the oil tanker's shape?

◄ For a yacht to go fast, it must be narrow in order to cut through the water. Try making a model yacht out of modeling clay with a straw mast and paper sail.

▼ Float your boat in the bathtub and blow on the sail. How can you make it go faster? See what happens if you change the shape of the sail and boat.

Surface tension

Something very interesting happens to the surface of water. You have to get very close and look carefully to see it.

▶ How many pins at a time can you put in a glass full to the brim with water without any water spilling over? You may think the answer is none. Try it! Drop pins in one at a time. How many can you fit in the glass: 5, 10, 20, 40? Look closely at the surface of the water. Instead of pouring out, the water seems to be held in by an invisible "skin." This is called surface tension.

▶ You might be surprised to find out how strong the skin on the surface of water is. Do you think it can support a pin even though the pin is made of metal? Carefully float a small piece of paper towel on water. Quickly drop a pin on it and watch what happens when the paper sinks. The pin is left on the water's surface. If you look closely, you should be able to see where the surface of the water is holding it up.

Pins are very sharp so be careful when you handle them!

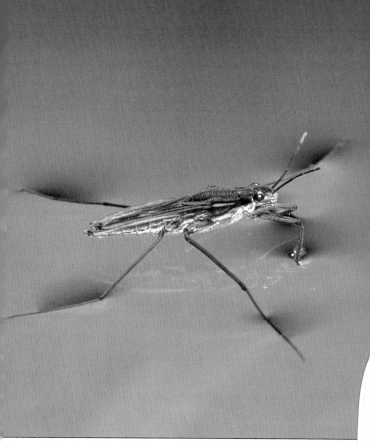

Some water insects, called pond skaters, can walk on water without getting their feet wet. Hairy pads on their legs trap bubbles of air and keep them afloat. Pond skaters can move across the surface of a body of water without breaking its "skin" and catch insects that have fallen into the water.

Separating colors

How black is black ink? Is it really made from mixing different colors? This experiment shows you how to use water to find out.

All you need is some white blotting paper, black ink, a glass, a pair of scissors, and, of course, some water.

▶ Cut a circle out of the blotting paper a bit larger than the top of the glass. Put a small blot of ink in the center of the blotting paper. Next, make two cuts in it (see right) and fold the middle strip down. Carefully place the blotting paper over the top of the glass with the thin strip in the water. Watch closely and you won't believe your eyes! As the water is slowly soaked up by the blotting paper, the ink separates into colors. This is called chromatography, which means "color drawing." Try it with different colored inks or food coloring to see what colors they are made of.

All-purpose water

We use water for all sorts of things around the house like washing, drinking, and watering plants. Wastewater from our homes is cleaned at a sewage plant. How many uses of water can you think of?

To be sure of a good water supply to people's houses all year round, **dams** can be built across **rivers** to make artificial **lakes** called **reservoirs**. In wet weather the reservoirs fill up and store water for use when there is less rain. All over the world, reservoirs are also used to store water for **irrigation**. In areas where there is little rainfall, local farmers can channel water to their fields.

Water is a source of power, too. Try holding your thumb over the end of a hose with water flowing out of it. If you take your thumb away, the water will gush out. This water force is used in **hydroelectric power stations** to produce **electricity**.

◄ Watermills use the force of falling water. The rushing water of a stream pours along a special channel and onto the blades of a huge water wheel at the side of a mill. As the wheel turns, it powers machinery inside the mill which grinds huge stones together. In the past, these mills were used to grind corn or wheat.

FastFact
About seven percent of the world's electricity is supplied by hydro-electric power stations.

Dams store water in reservoirs high up in the mountains. Big pipes bring the water gushing downhill to hydroelectric power stations. There, the water pushes against the blades of a turbine. As the turbine spins quickly, it works the generator and makes electricity.

Falling water can be used to provide electricity to light whole cities.

Make your own water wheel

Here is an experiment to get power from moving water. You will need some cardboard, an old thread spool, a straw, and some double-sided tape.

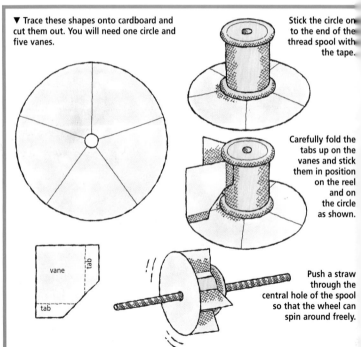

▼ Trace these shapes onto cardboard and cut them out. You will need one circle and five vanes.

Stick the circle on to the end of the thread spool with the tape.

Carefully fold the tabs up on the vanes and stick them in position on the reel and on the circle as shown.

vane

tab

tab

Push a straw through the central hole of the spool so that the wheel can spin around freely.

◀ Try spinning the wheel in the kitchen sink under running water from the faucet. Where does it spin fastest? When it is near the faucet's spout or further down the stream of water? Why do you think this is? Where is the water moving fastest?

Being water aware

As the number of people on the Earth increases, more and more clean water is needed. We must be careful not to waste our supply. The **rivers** and **lakes** where our clean water comes from have to be protect from **pollution**.

...rmful substances need to be removed ...m waste before it is poured into rivers or ...eans. At home, you can protect the water ...ply by using less water and not pouring ...isons down the drain. Cleaning wastewater ...make it usable again is a long and ...pensive process.

FastFact
About 12 percent of a city's water supply is lost through leaky pipes and faucets in homes.

...Waste released from factories and ...emicals used in farming sometimes enter ...e water supply and cause pollution in ...ers and oceans. This can make the water ...healthy for fish and other sea creatures.

◄ In some places around the world there is no regular supply of clean, running water and there is a danger of water spreading disease. In many less developed countries where there is often less rainfall, water has to be carried home over long distances. Much of this water comes straight from rivers or deep wells.

Saving water

Even though the Earth is covered with water, we can only use about three percent of this for drinking or cleaning. We have to collect rainwater and clean it for use at home. Many parts of the world get a lot of rainfall. But in dry areas, or during dry weather, the level of rainwater collected in **reservoirs** can drop so low that water shortages occur, so we must be careful not to waste water. Use the water survey on page 32 to see how much water you use and follow the tips on these pages to save water.

Shower
About a quarter of the water used at home is used in showers and baths. A quick shower uses a lot less water than a bath. Save water by turning off the shower while you shampoo your hair.

Dripping faucet
If a faucet drips once every second, it wastes about 3 gallons (14 liters) of water in a day. Dripping faucets should be fixed!

Bath
It takes about 24 gallons (90 liters) of water to fill a bathtub.

Toilet
Three gallons (11 liters) of water are used to flush an old toilet. The amount of water can be reduced by using a tank with a short or long flush choice or by putting a brick, or a bottle filled with water, in the tank.

Brushing your teeth
A running faucet releases about 2 gallons (9 liters) of water every minute. Turning off the faucet while brushing your teeth can save about 5 gallons (20 liters) of water a day. After brushing, try rinsing your mouth with water from a paper cup.

Sink
Put the stopper in the drain before turning on the faucet. Run a little water into the sink and use this for washing rather than leaving a running faucet.

...eaning
...ater is used to
...ean the house, to
...ash surfaces,
...op floors, and
...ean windows.

...iling an egg
...hen you boil an
...g, save the cooled
...ater for house
...ants. The eggshell
...eases useful
...emicals that plants
...n feed on!

...ashing food
...ashing food under
...running faucet uses
...gallons (9 liters) of
...ater every minute.

House plants
Like all plants, house
plants need water to
survive, but some,
such as cacti, need a
lot less than others.

Washing machine
Most washing
machine cycles
use 25 gallons
(955 liters)
of water.

Drinks
A person may drink
more than 15,000
gallons (60,600 liters)
of water during his
or her lifetime!

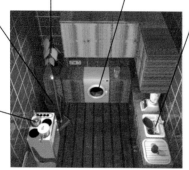

Washing dishes
On average, 10
gallons (38 liters)
of water are used
in one wash in a
dish washer. Not
everyone enjoys
washing dishes by
hand, but washing
them in the sink
uses less water
and **electricity**
than a dishwasher.

...ashing the car
...ashing cars keeps them looking clean and
...akes it easier to see any areas of damage
...r rust on them. Each bucket of water
...ontains about 2 gallons
... liters).

...awn sprinkler
... lawn sprinkler can
...se as much water in
...n hour as a family of
...our uses in a day! A
...arden hose releases
...bout 30 gallons (125
...ters) of water every
...5 minutes.

Outdoor plants
In dry weather, outdoor plants will need
watering regularly. If you have a **fish tank**,
when you change the water, use the old
water to water
plants. Chemicals
in the water from
fish tanks make it
a good **fertilizer**.

Outdoors
A family with a
yard may use
half of all their
water outdoors.

Survey

**Photocopy and fill in this water survey to keep a record
of how much water you use every day.**

How much do you drink each
day? (All of these drinks are
made up mostly of water.)

Canned or bottled drinks......... ☐

Glasses of water/milk/
soft drinks............................ ☐

Cups of hot chocolate/other
hot drinks............................ ☐

How many times a day
do you brush your teeth? ☐

How many times a day
do you wash?

Sink.................................... ☐

Shower................................ ☐

Bath.................................... ☐

How many times a day
do you flush a toilet? ☐

How many times a week
is a washing machine used? ☐

How many times a day
are dishes cleaned? ☐

Are they cleaned by hand or with
a dishwasher?

....

How many times a week is
water used to clean the house? ☐

Other possible uses. How
many times a month do you...

Wash a car............................ ☐

Water a garden or lawn .... ☐

Water indoor plants................ ☐

Find out if you have a water meter in
your house and take readings to see
how much water is used each week.

Week 1................................
Week 2................................
Week 3................................

Puzzles

Photocopy this page to write n your answers.

1. You have a jug that holds 4 gallons (5 liters) of water and a jug that holds 3 gallons (4 liters) of water. Use them to measure out exactly 2 gallons (3 liters). How do you do this?

2. Which of these doesn't belong?
   a) The Nile River
   b) Loch Ness
   c) Sea of Tranquility
   d) Niagara Falls
   e) The Suez Canal

3. Water word wheel
   A lot of sports take place in water and on ice. How many can you find in the water wheel below? Do you know which are water sports and which are snow and ice sports?

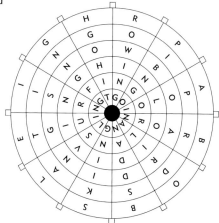

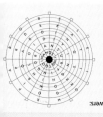

33

Glossary

boiling When a liquid turns into a gas by heating. Water boils at 212°F (100°C) at sea level.

chromatography A way of separating a mixture to find out what it is made of.

clouds Condensed water droplets or ice crystals that are held in the air.

condensation When a gas or vapor turns into a liquid by cooling.

dam A man-made blockage or wall holding back water.

electricity A type of energy used to make bulbs light up, turn motors, etc.

energy Power needed for all activity.

evaporation When a liquid turns into a gas or vapor.

fertilizer A mixture that is added to soil or water to help plants grow.

fish A cold-blooded animal that lives in water. Fish have fins for swimming and gills for breathing.

floating Resting on the surface of water.

fog Condensed water droplets that float near the ground making it difficult to see

force The power to move an object.

gas An airlike substance, which flows free to fill any space.

groundwater Water that falls as rain and is soaked up by the soil.

hail Small lumps of ice that fall from clouds. These are also known as hailstones

hydroelectric power station A building where electricity is made by falling water pushed through turbines.

ice Water that is frozen. Water freezes at 32°F (0°C) at sea level.

ect An animal with an external skeleton, ennae, three pairs of legs, and usually gs. Flies, ants, and crickets are all insects.

gation A way of moving water to dry as using canals or ditches. It is often used farmers.

e A large, natural body of water rounded by land.

uid A waterlike substance, flowing freely, always with the same volume.

mmal A warm-blooded animal usually th hair or fur. Female mammals feed their young with milk. Humans, dogs, cats, and whales are all mammals.

marine To do with the ocean. A marine biologist is a biologist who is mainly interested in ocean life.

minerals Non-living substances which all living things need to survive. We take in minerals from the food we eat and from the water we drink. Minerals are also found in rocks and may be mined.

ocean A large body of water, especially the Atlantic, Pacific, Indian, Arctic and Antarctic Oceans.

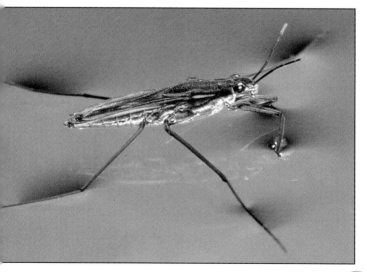

oil A thick liquid, found in animals, plants, and minerals. Oil is used for cooking and as fuel for transportation and machinery.

particle A tiny amount of something.

pollution Harmful substances that get into the environment.

pressure The weight of an object on an are

reservoir A man-made lake used for collecting rainwater.

river A large amount of water flowing ov land to the ocean or a lake and carving a channel for itself.

roots The parts of a plant that grow underground. Roots take in water and help stop the plant from falling over.

sinking Falling in a liquid. When a boat is unable to float on water, it sinks.

snow Frozen water falling from clouds to the ground in crystals.

solid A rocklike quality that is firm and stable in shape and volume.

stream A small river. A river usually starts as a stream, widens to become a river, and ends in an ocean.

submarine A vessel that is specially designed to travel underwater.

submerge To sink below the water's surface. Submarines travel submerged.

sugar A sweet substance found in plants and used for energy.

surface tension The invisible "skin" on the surface of water.

turbine A spinning motor that is pushed around by moving water or steam.

valley A low area usually enclosed by hills with a stream flowing through it.

volcano A mountain that has an opening in the Earth's crust. Lava, steam, gases, and other materials escape from this opening.

volume The space that an object takes up.

water cycle The movement of water from the ocean to the clouds, then to rain and rivers and back to the ocean again.

water vapor Water found in the atmosphere or air.

weight The force with which something pushes downward.

well A hole in the ground from which we take water or oil. Wells can be natural or manufactured.

yacht A sailing boat built especially for cruising or racing.

Workbook

Photocopy this sheet and use it to make your own note

Workbook

Photocopy this sheet and use it to make your own note

Draw your own water scene

Questions and answers

Water travels a long way, from the **ocean** up to the **clouds** as **water vapor** and back down as rain. It then flows down hills as **streams** and **rivers**, forms **lakes** and swamps and one way or another ends up back in the ocean. Millions of creatures live in watery surroundings, and Claude the Hermit Crab and Shelly the Turtle are just two of them. See if they can answer all your questions about the substance that is their home.

How much of the Earth is covered by water?
More than 70 percent of the planet Earth is covered by oceans and seas. The oceans are one huge expanse of water, while seas are smaller and usually surrounded by land. Ocean water is too salty to drink. The sun heats up the surface of the water and turns it into a **gas** called water vapor. This process is called evaporation. When ocean water **evaporates**, the salt is left behind.

Turtles are related to tortoises, but live in water instead of on land.

Shelly the Turtle

How much water is in the air?
Only one-thousandth of one percent of the Earth's water is found in the air at any one time. When water vapor reaches a certain height, it cools down to form tiny drops of liquid water. This process is known as **condensation**.

How do clouds form?
When water vapor cools down to form droplets high above the Earth's surface, the water collects around very tiny **particle** of dust. These tiny drops of water floating in the sky form clouds. Clouds form at different heights. In the highest clouds, the water droplets are so cold they often freeze into **ice**.

What are rivers made of?
Rivers are made of rainwater. They often start high up in hills and mountains. As the flow downhill, they take in water from streams or other rivers until they reach a large river, a lake, or the ocean. The longes river in the world is the Nile. It is 4,145 mile (6,741km) long and flows from Burundi in east-central Africa to Egypt in North Africa.

How much water do trees drink?
A fully grown apple tree can take in 95 gallons (360 liters) of water from the soil every day! Rain pours down to Earth and seeps into the soil. The trees take in water through their **roots**. This water then travels around inside the tree carrying usefu **minerals** and **sugars** which help the trees to grow.

at is groundwater?

water that lands on the ground, but
ot taken in by tree **roots**, is called
undwater. Some of the rainfall is soaked
by rocks and soil. This builds up into a
ply of water underground called
undwater. Groundwater soaks through
soil eventually reaching rivers, lakes,
oceans. Even when it hasn't rained
a long time, this groundwater supply
keep rivers flowing.

w are reservoirs made?

servoirs are usually made by building
lls around part of a **valley** or digging
ge holes in the ground. They store water
our use and can also be used to prevent
oding. The world's largest artificially
ated reservoir is the Bratskoye reservoir
Russia. It covers an area of 3,400 square
es (5,470 square km) and can hold
million cubic feet (169 cubic km) of water.

cities use much water?

each person living in a city, an average
10 gallons (38 liters) of water is used on
eet cleaning and firefighting every day!

here does the salt in the ocean come from?

ean salt comes from fresh water rivers.
e fresh water flowing in rivers and streams
rries salts from the soil to the ocean. Because
is has been happening for a very long time,
e ocean has become quite salty. The Dead
a, a giant lake between Israel and Jordan, is
ore salty than any ocean because its water
aporates in the sun and leaves only salt.

Hermit crabs
are crabs that
live in the
cast-off shells
of other
animals.

Claude the
Hermit Crab

Is there only fresh water and salt water?

There are many areas of water that are not
as salty as the ocean, but could not be called
fresh water either. They include many
swamps and marshes, areas near the coast,
and other places where evaporation has
caused the salt content of the water to
become higher than usual. This kind of
water is called brackish.

What is a water clock?

A water clock is a clock that uses the flow of
water to measure time.

Who were the mythical gods of the ocean?

For the ancient Greeks, Poseidon was the
god of the ocean. The Roman god of the
ocean was Neptune. Romans made offerings
to Neptune to bring fresh water as well as
ocean water to help them to grow crops.

Are there any mythical creatures connected with fresh water?

In Greek mythology, female spirits called naiads
were said to live in lakes, fountains, rivers, or
streams. They were thought to be kind to
people and to live for thousands of years.

Index

A
Archimedes 14

C
chromatography 22
clouds 6, 8, 9, 44
condensation 6, 7, 9, 44

D
dam 24–25

E
electricity 25
evaporation 6, 44

F
floating 16–17, 18, 19, 20, 21
fog 9

H
hail 9
hydroelectric power station 24, 25

I
ice 4, 5, 9, 33, 44
irrigation 24

N
naiads 45
Neptune 45

O
oceans 4, 6, 12, 44, 45
oil tanker 18–19

...lution 28, 29
...seidon 45

...n 6, 8, 24, 44
...ervoir 24, 25, 45

...king 16–17, 20
...ow 9
...am 4
...bmarine 12–13
...rface tension 20–21

...rbine 25

V
volume 14–15

W
water clock 45
water cycle 6–7, 44–45
water power 24, 25, 26, 27
water uses 24
water vapor 4, 6, 8, 9, 44
water wheel 25, 26–27
weather 8–9, 44–45
weight 14–15

www.two-canpublishing.com

Published by Two-Can Publishing LLC
234 Nassau Street, Princeton, NJ 08542

For information on Two-Can books and multimedia, call
1-609-021-6700, fax 1-609-921-3349, or visit our Web site.

ISBN 1-58728-761-7

1 2 3 4 5 6 7 8 9 10 03 02 01

Photograph credits: All photographs are © Fiona Pragoff, except for the following:
Cosmo Condina/Tony Stone Images: front cover; Science Photo Library: p.4 (t&br);
Pictor International: p.4 (bl); Zefa Picture Library (UK) Ltd: p.5, p.10, p.18, p.29 (t);
Oxford Scientific Films: p.8; Frank Lane Picture Agency: p.8 (inset), p.9 (c);
Ardea: p.9 (t&b), p.24, p.25 (b); Bruce Coleman Ltd: p.12, p.21, p.25 (t);
Tony Stone Images: p.28, p.29.
All illustrations are by Sally Kindberg, except those on pp.30–31
and pp.44–45 which are by Michele Egar, Sarah Evans, Frog and Jon Stuart.

Every effort has been made to acknowledge correctly and contact the source of each
picture and Two-Can Publishing apologises for any unintentional errors or omissions
which will be corrected in future editions of this book.

Printed in Hong Kong by Wing King Tong

This title previously published in a large format.